Fly Casting

ILLUSTRATED IN COLOR

Photography: Jim Schollmeyer

Text: Frank Amato and Jim Schollmeyer

Frank
Amato

PORTLAND

Softbound ISBN: 1-878175-56-4

Published in 1993 by Frank Amato Publications, Box 82112, Portland, Oregon 97282

Book Design: Tony Amato

Printed in Hong Kong
10 9 8 7 6 5 4 3 2

Contents

Author, photographer Jim Scollmeyer.

Asthetics

The Sensual Pleasure of Fly Casting:
If It Feels Good, You've Got It Down

Do you remember how good it felt as a care-free kid to accurately throw a dirt clod or rock, or skip a flat stone across a water surface, or pitch a baseball? Fly casting offers that kind of pleasure as well as grace, beauty and rhythm. A fly rod seems to come alive in your hand as it pulses on the forward and back cast. The sensation is physically and mentally relaxing, felt into your shoulder and your psyche, and in no time at all you are light-years away from the concerns of your otherwise busy mind. It is now just you and the fish and the pleasant sensation of casting in a beautiful stream environment. It just plain feels good to cast a fly rod.

To cast efficiently, however, you must get a feel for the rod and line. Nerves, muscles and brain must communicate, become coordinated, and learn the timing. But with practice the motion and rhythm will become second nature, a kind of pleasant instinct that comes by itself. You'll know you have it when it feels just right. Even on those days when you get skunked—and they happen—it doesn't feel so bad knowing that you've cast well. Casting and fishing a fly properly are their own reward.

The Challenge of Fly Casting

There is more to fly casting than simply laying out the line. It must be done with a smoothness and efficiency that will not alarm the fish. All their lives trout are continually hunted by predators. Wild trout eggs are eaten by sculpin; fingerlings are attacked by kingfishers and mergansers; adult trout are captured by ospreys, otters and fishermen. Trout survive because they are constantly on the lookout for these dangers.

The object of fly casting is to quietly place the fly near the fish without arousing its natural suspicion and spooking it. The angler must understand the best places to cast from, and position himself to minimize obstacles—trees, brush and conflicting currents—without being seen. In this respect fly fishing can be thought of as hunting, where every move must be stealthy and considered in advance.

The fisherman must also understand water. Flat, clear water demands especially precise and delicate casting to keep from alarming the fish. Riffles make it harder for the trout to see above the surface, and harder for predators to see beneath it. Broken water is a much easier situation for fishermen, and often allows different casts and presentations.

But in order to benefit from the understanding of casting position and water types, the fisherman must learn the several casting methods presented in this book. Like baseball and golf, fly fishing is a sport of position and execution. These different casts will allow you to take the best advantage of almost all fishing situations.

The accurate fly caster and knowledgeable fisherman will enjoy many fish hooked through the season. But perhaps one of the greatest beauties of fly fishing is the intense visual relationship with nature, and the fact that the object of your desire can be released unharmed to reproduce and provide pleasure for other fishermen.

1
Tackle

Fly Rods:
Length and Casting Action

Fly rods vary in length from 5 to over 15 feet or more, but I prefer to use rods between 7 to 10 feet long. For the beginner (and expert as well), an 8 1/2 or 9 foot rod will handle virtually all trout and bass fishing.

Rods of this length carry different line-weight ratings, and choosing the right one depends upon fish species and water types. As a general rule if you plan to fish for trout on small streams, I suggest an 8 to 9 foot, #3, #4 or #5-weight rod. If you plan to fish larger streams where longer casts are needed, or in lakes for bass, I recommend a 9 foot, #6 or #7-weight rod. The rod should match the fishing conditions, so it's best to consult a fly-angling friend or better yet, visit a fly shop. This is the most reliable and accurate source of information.

Fast action rod

Slow action rod

Neither length nor line weight has a direct bearing on rod action. Action is solely a function of the rod taper and the material from which it is made—whether bamboo, fiberglass or graphite. A fast-action rod is stiffer in the mid-section with a softer tip. It will cast more quickly and a bit farther in the wind because its mid-rod strength delivers more speed and helps create a tighter, less wind-resistant loop. A fast-action rod is best for casts of 40 to 80 feet, and I prefer them for steelhead and other large fish that require long casts and large flies. At shorter distances, though, the stiffness makes the rod less pleasurable to cast than one with a slower action. I prefer a slower casting rod for trout because it gives me more casting pleasure, though with experience it can still be cast long distances. The choice of rod action is yours, but because it is an important one, again I refer you to an informed friend or local fly shop.

Fly Reels

In fly fishing, the reel plays no direct part in the dynamics of the cast. Instead, the primary function is to store the fly line. With your free hand (also called the "line hand" as opposed to the "rod hand") you strip line off the reel in order to cast, and wind it back on the reel when you're finished casting. A good reel will not overrun and tangle when you strip off line. Big fish make extra demands on a reel, particularly reels fitted with drags. Spools should fit securely on the spindle and not wobble when a big fish runs. The drag should operate smoothly, with an even progression from light to strong. The bigger the fish you expect to hook, the greater the need for a high-quality reel.

Fly Line Backing

I strongly recommend you purchase a fly reel that will hold 50 to 100 yards of backing in addition to the fly line. Braided backing in the 20 to 30 lb. range will allow the fly line to fill the spool in large coils and reduce line memory caused by smaller line coils. The backing will also let you wind in line at a faster rate because of the larger effective diameter created by the backing. And if you hook a large fish, the backing will be there when it's needed.

Fly Lines: Floating and Sinking; Double Tapered and Weight-Forward

Floating lines are designed to ride on the surface of the water, and they offer the best control of the fly, whether on or under the water. Certain line-handling techniques (like line mending) and certain casts (like the roll cast) are performed most easily with this type of line. Floating lines need no line dressing, but to keep them floating properly you should clean them periodically.

Sink-tip or full-sinking lines are heavier than water and are designed to fish a fly underwater. You can vary the depth at which the fly is fished by timing the interval in which you let it sink.

This book is intended to help you learn to cast with a floating line, which is generally the most useful for most fishing situations. Casting sinking lines is more difficult, and is best learned by first mastering floating lines. In the following pages, however, I will provide tips concerning the casting of sinking lines when I think it will help you.

A fly line provides the weight that loads the rod. If the weight is distributed uniformly along the length of the line, the line diameter remains constant. This is called a "level line," and they are seldom used. A fly line that is thicker and heavier near the tip, and tappers to a thin diameter farther back, is called a "weight-forward line". In my personal fishing I use a weight-forward floating line because I often need casts of 40 to 75 feet on wide Western rivers that are often windy. Because of its design, the weight-forward line lets you cast farther and more easily into the wind.

A line that is thickest and heaviest at the middle, and tappers to a thinner diameter at both ends is called a "double-taper line". Though it will not cast as far as a weight-forward line, the double taper is a very smooth casting line that delivers the fly gently on casts of 10 to 40 feet, which makes it better on trout streams where shorter, more delicate casts are often in order. A double-taper line also gives you two lines for the price of one; when one end of the line wears out, you can simply reverse it. This is not possible with weight-forward lines since they are not symmetrical.

I have found, as a general rule, that a rod designated by a manufacturer to cast a #6 line will cast a #6 double taper, but not so well a #6 weight-forward. If you are going to use a weight forward line, I suggest that you go up one line size from that recomended on the rod.

Fly Lines

To Backing   To Leader

Level

Weight Forward

Double Taper

Shooting Head

Saltwater Type

Leaders, Tippets and Fly Size

A leader transfers the energy of the fly line down to the fly, and provides a smaller-diameter, inconspicuous line to tie your fly to. Like fly lines, leaders are tapered, and they are designated by a tippet size that balances with specific sizes of flies.

The tippet is the uniform-diameter section of material at the end of the leader. Since this section is usually rather long, from 24 to 36 inches, it helps give the fly a more natural drift and allows you to change flies many times before the tippet requires replacement.

Tippet size should be chosen to balance the size of the fly. Large flies, from #2 to #8, require large-diameter tippets—1x, 2x or 3x. Medium size flies, from #10 to #16, require mid-size tippets—3x, 4x or 5x. Smaller flies need finer tippets, 5x or 6x. Care in balancing leader, tippet and fly makes for easy, trouble-free casting.

Glasses

Polarized sun glasses should be worn not only to protect your eyes from the sun but to help you see better through the water. The improved visibility around and beneath the water can help you understand its currents and so improve line control and fly drift. Because polarized glasses cut glare, they make it easier to follow the fly and fly line, and to see strikes. Glasses are also an important protection against an injury caused by your fly.

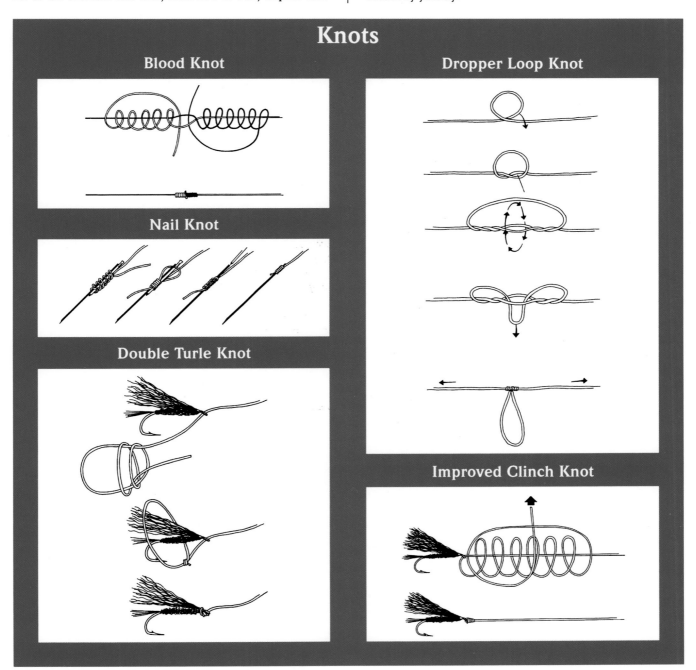

Knots

Blood Knot

Dropper Loop Knot

Nail Knot

Double Turle Knot

Improved Clinch Knot

2
Preparation for Casting

Stringing the Fly Rod

To thread the fly line through the rod guides, begin by stripping out a length of fly line two feet longer than the rod. Now double the fly line one foot back from the leader, forming a small loop. This loop is easier to thread through the rod guides than the small end of the leader.

Holding the Rod

1. *Hold the handle in the center, with the thumb on top of the grip and parallel to the rod. This thumb position allows maximum power during the cast and helps prevent you from dropping the rod too far down on the backcast.*

Your free hand (the left hand if you're right-handed) controls the fly line during the various stages of fishing and casting. Hold a loose coil of fly line in this hand. This will keep the line taut, making it possible to strike quickly if a fish hits or minimize slack when you're ready to cast.

2. *On a very short cast of up to 20 feet, you can hold the line by pinching it between the thumb and forefinger. But on longer casts, hold the line as shown in the previous photograph.*

3. *If you wish to strip in some line—to work the fly in the water or to make another cast—simply place the line over the forefinger of your rod hand . . .*

4. *. . . and pull down with your left hand. To continue stripping in line, pinch the line against the rod handle with your forefinger. With your left hand, grasp the line directly behind the right forefinger, and pull down on the line again. Continue this "pinch-and-pull" until you have stripped in the desired amount of line.*

Where and How to Start Casting

If no pond or river is nearby, practice casting on the grass. Avoid paved surfaces because they can crack the exterior of the fly line. When practicing the roll cast you can wet the grass to increase the resistance on the line which better imitates the feel of the cast on water.

For practice, tie a 3/4 inch piece of bright yarn on the end of your leader instead of a fly. The yarn will make it easy to spot where the cast is landing. When the casting begins to feel more natural, place targets at different distances to improve your accuracy.

Getting the Line Out

Strip 5 to 10 feet of line off the reel, pull it through the guides, and lay it out in front of you. Then pull more line off the reel, enough for a 20 or 25 foot cast. With the rod tip pointed toward the ground, wiggle the rod tip back and forth about 2 to 3 feet. This motion will pull the slack line from the coils at your feet, draw it through the guides, and deposit it off the end of the rod onto the water or grass. The process is made simpler if you use your left hand to lift the line from the ground and "feed" it into the first guide on the fly rod.

The ability to feed out line comes in handy in situations where you need additional slack on the water. For example, a trout is rising beneath a bush downstream of you. A conventional cast won't get the fly underneath the brush. So just place your fly, leader and several feet of line on the water; strip enough line off the reel to reach the fish, and then let the fly and slack line float freely down to the trout while you wiggle your rod tip to feed out the extra line through the guides.

Posture

Years ago, the wonderful nuns in grade school used to tell me constantly, "Sit up Frank!" as I slouched at my desk. How right they were, and I will repeat the same advice to you, "Stand up straight when casting and fishing the fly!" By standing erect through the angling day you'll avoid muscle strain in your shoulders and back. If you're not in the best shape then it's a good idea to train yourself to hold your stomach in when fishing. This keeps the back muscles from straining and helps you avoid back pain.

The exception to good posture occurs on small trout streams where standing upright may make you visible to the fish. In this situation you may want to bend or kneel to keep a low profile and prevent spooking the fish. Kneeling is preferable to hunching over since it places less strain on the back.

Eyes in the Back of Your Head:

Good fly casters rarely snag on the backcast because they turn around and look for any obstacles that may be behind them. They do this by putting the left foot forward and standing at an angle that allows them to see over their right shoulder. This position lets you watch your backcast and direct it away from trouble. When practicing make it a habit to watch your backcast because a good backcast is necessary for a good forward cast.

We've come a ways from the line piled up in front of your rod, so let's get back to it. If you are in moving water the current will pull the line downstream. But on still water or on grass the line will just lay there until you move it with a roll cast.

3
Roll Casts

The roll cast is used when you can't make an overhead cast because of trees, brush or cliffs behind you. You will use it often. The roll-casting motion also has a variety of applications other then delivery of the fly. You can roll the line forward to pick up slack coiled at your feet; to pick up line for an overhead cast; and to roll a sink-tip line forward to raise it out of the water in preparation for another cast.

To execute the roll cast properly you should have from 20 to 25 feet of fly line laid out on the grass or water. The line should be lying out in front of you and about 3 feet to the side of your right leg.

1. Draw the rod slowly up and back. Stop briefly at the 1 o'clock position (think of the rod as an hour hand on a clock off your right shoulder) and allow the fly line to come to a complete stop.

2. Come down smartly and thrust forward with your forearm. As the rod reaches the 11 o'clock position, drive the rod down with your wrist, as if the rod were a hammer and you were hitting a nail. Then abruptly stop at the 9 o'clock position, this will cause a loop to form off the end of the rod.

3. If you have exerted enough power at the proper time, the loop will roll forward in front of you . . .

4. . . . landing in a straight line. Casts of 40 feet or more can easily be made this way. The roll cast is easiest in slow water. In fast water you must draw the line back and make the cast in a fairly quick, continuous motion or the current will drag the trailing line out of position. On windy days the roll cast is easiest and most useful if you can get the wind to your back. Under such conditions it is possible to achieve shooting roll casts of up to 60 feet.

Shooting-line Roll Cast

1. Once you become comfortable with the roll cast you can use the shooting-line cast to achieve greater distance. Strip off 5 or 10 feet of extra line and hold it in your left hand. Begin by making the usual roll cast.

2. As the line begins to straighten out in front let go of the extra line in your left hand and . . .

3. . . . it will shoot out, extending the cast up to 5 to 10 feet or more.

Aerial Roll Cast

To execute the aerial roll cast the rod is aimed high on the power stroke and stopped at the 10 or 11 o'clock position. This will cause the line to roll out in the air rather than on the water. This is a good cast for shooting extra line or casting when the wind is behind you.

Off-shoulder Roll Cast

1. This is a handy roll cast when brush or obstructions on your rod-hand side make the standard roll cast impossible. Simply bring the rod across your body and over your opposite shoulder and proceed as you would with a normal cast. Quickly, but carefully, raise the rod with the line extending straight out from you . . .

2. . . . and then come down smartly as if hitting a nail. Make certain that the rod comes down to the right of the fly line to avoid tangles.

3. The cast completed.

4
Basic Casts

When practicing, deliver the casting strokes with the same motions as throwing a football or darts. Move your forearm in and out so that your casting hand travels in a straight line at eye level. Lock your wrist, with the thumb parallel to the forearm, so that the rod points straight up when your arm is in the 12 o'clock position. Try not to bend your wrist until the end of the casting stroke. Using your wrist in the middle of the casting stroke will widen the line loop and shorten your casting distance.

At the beginning of each stroke start slowly to make the line move in the direction of the rod, then increase your arm speed, again just like throwing a dart. After the rod is loaded—normally in the 10 o'clock position on the forward cast and the 12 to 1 o'clock position on the backcast—give a quick flick of the wrist in the direction of the cast to drop the tip out of the fly line's path. Then abruptly stop the rod. Stopping the rod causes the loop to form in the line. The size of the loop is determined by the amount of wrist movement you use. More bend in the wrist means larger, more open loops; less bend means smaller, tighter loops.

When casting, aim the fly for a point 2 feet above the grass (or water) and try to keep the backcast and forward casts in the same plane by moving the casting hand in a straight line rather than an arc.

The Basic Overhead Cast

1. To make the basic overhead cast strip out about 25 feet of line beyond your rod tip and lay it in front of you on the grass or water. Lower the rod tip to provide a straight pull from the rod to fly line and hold a small loop of line in your left hand. Using your forearm and locked wrist . . .

2. . . . lift the rod with a smooth flow of power that starts out slow and increases sharply as the rod is lifted. After the line has left the water . . .

3. . . . give the rod a final burst of power by snapping your wrist a few degrees to the rear, like throwing a dart backwards. Then abruptly stop the rod at the 1 o'clock position. This sudden stop will form a loop off the tip of the rod.

4. Letting the rod drift back slightly as the line straightens out will lengthen the distance of your forward stroke for a smooth flowing cast. When the line is almost fully extended behind you . . .

5. . . . begin the forward cast. Lock your wrist and move your forearm forward in a straight line, again starting slowly and increasing your speed. The line will start forward, following the rod tip exactly, and remain in the same plane as the backcast. If you start forward too soon the line will crack like a whip; if you start to late the fly line will drop too low and result in an inefficient forward cast. Once the forearm is completely extended the line moves forward rapidly.

6. *The wrist has just applied its forward burst of power, like throwing a dart forward, and the rod is loaded and ready to release this stored energy. Now the rod has stopped . . .*

7. *. . . and transferred its energy into the moving line to form the start of a casting loop. The rod tip has been lowered, opening the loop to keep the line from running into itself as it rolls forward. The rod tip . . .*

8. . . . is following the fly line down as the line extends outward. If you aim at an imaginary point 2 feet above the water's surface, the line will unroll in the air, parallel to the water, and then line, leader and fly will fall lightly on the surface without a noisy splash. Practice will familiarize you with the timing necessary for such a cast.

Target Point In Air

X

False Cast

At the end of the forward cast, as the line straightens out, you can start the casting cycle over again by making a backcast rather than letting the line land on the water. This is called false casting.

The false cast is used to extend line—you shoot a little line just as the forward cast and backcast straightens out. False casting will also help dry a waterlogged dry fly and can be used to change casting direction. Finally, holding the line in the air by false casting will keep it from tangling when you walk or wade a few feet to a new casting position.

Single Haul or Pick Up

If the fly line is not straight on the water or if you have more line out than the rod can lift off the water efficiently, use the single haul. The single haul will straighten the line and start it moving toward you, which allows you to make an efficient cast without overloading the rod.

1. Lower the rod tip to the water. With your left hand, pinch the line next to the stripping guide (the first guide up from the rod handle). As you start to lift the rod for the start of your backcast . . .

2. ... pull (or "haul") on the line at the same speed as you lift the rod. The length of the pull will depend on the amount of line on the water. A long line requires a long pull; a short line, a shorter pull. The end of the fly line must leave the water before the rod reaches 10 o'clock or the rod will not load properly. If this occurs, the backcast will not straighten behind you, which in turn will cause your forward cast to fall in a pile in front of you.

Double Haul

The double haul will make your casts easier and more efficient. This cast consists of pulling on the fly line with your left hand during both the forward cast and backcast. These additional pulls create substantially higher line speeds. If used with a narrow casting loop, the double haul can extend your cast up to 20 feet or more and can also help you cast into stiff winds. Even at shorter distances, the double haul is useful in helping to maintain a taut fly line, which improves your line control under the wide variety of casting conditions encountered in a day's fishing.

1. To double haul, start with the single haul to lift the line off the water . . .

2. . . . as the line is straightening behind you, with the rod in the 1 o'clock position . . .

3. . . . move your line hand up toward the stripping guide. The pull of the extending line will keep slack out of the line between your hand and the stripping guide.

4. Start the forward cast with the same smooth increase of power used in the basic cast and at the same time pull down ("haul") with the line hand, matching the smooth motion of your casting arm. If you pull too hard or jerk on the line during the haul it will send shock waves down the line or cause the line to tangle.

With the line speed increased by the second or "double haul" on the forward cast, the extra line coiled in your hand will jump out of your hand when it is released at the completion of the forward cast.

If you want to continue the double haul, hold on to the line and move the line hand back toward the stripping guide at the end of the forward cast. Then start the cycle over again.

You can feed line out the guides as the line extends in the forward cast and backcast. This is an excellent way to extend the length of your cast.

Casting Angle

The most efficient casting angle is 180 degrees (or a straight line) regardless of how much it's tilted, which occurs when you change casting distances or cast into or with the wind.

But if there is an obstruction behind you, such as a sloping bank or brush and you have to make a high backcast with a level forward cast, then the casting angle changes to a narrower angle and the cast becomes less efficient, which shortens your casting distance.

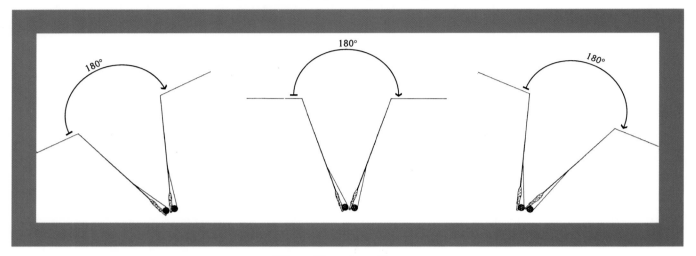

The Casting Loop

When you cast a fly rod, the fly line follows exactly the motion of the rod tip. When you stop the movement of the rod at the end of a backcast or forward cast, the trailing fly line will roll past the fly rod tip and continue in the direction that the rod has been moving. The "U" shape the fly line creates as it unrolls past the rod tip is called a "casting loop."

If the rod tip travels in a straight line and is not moved out of the way after it stops, the fly line will run into the tip of the rod. To prevent this from happening, lower the tip of the rod at the end of the cast. The more the rod tip is lowered, the wider the loop becomes.

A narrow loop travels faster and more efficiently down the fly line and creates less air resistance, making a narrow loop ideal for casting long distances or fishing in windy conditions. A wide casting loop is less efficient and will not travel far or buck the wind well. But if a soft presentation of a dry fly, or casting a weighted nymph is necessary, then use a wide casting loop.

Remember, the fly line follows the direction of the rod tip during the casting stroke. If the rod tip moves in a wide arc through its casting stroke, you will not be able to form a narrow casting loop. Try to keep the fly line traveling in a straight line until the end of the casting stroke, and then open the loop by dropping the rod tip. In fact, the rod tip will normally drop slightly as you apply the final bit of power to the cast with your wrist at the end of the cast.

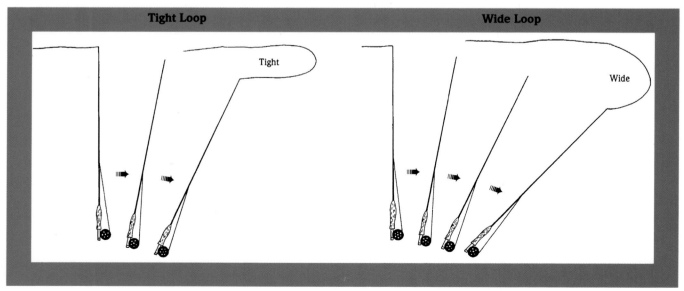

5
Specialty Casts

Mending Line to Control the Fly:
Trout Do Not Like The Dramatic

Mending is the art of manipulating the fly line on the water once the cast is completed. As soon as the fly line settles on the current, you have lost control of your fly's drift unless you continue to reposition the line on the water, thus changing the amount and direction of the drag affecting your fly. As a rule, trout don't like to chase their food downstream, near the surface, because it exposes them to predators. Trout prefer food that drifts with the current and behaves like the natural insect. Dramatic, unnatural movement, such as a fly dragging rapidly across the surface, will alarm the fish.

Mending is easiest with a floating line. The cleaner the line, the higher it floats, and the easier it is to mend. The sim-

plest way to mend is by lifting the amount of line you want to mend straight up off the water with your rod, and then gently moving the line with the rod held high, in the direction you want to mend the line.

If you try to mend without lifting the line off the water you will cause the fly to drag in the direction of the mend.

There are many advanced mending techniques you will learn as you spend more time on the water. But it's much better to control the drift of the fly with a cast that puts you and the fly in the best positions, and this will help keep mending to a minimum.

1. On moving water, as soon as the cast is completed a belly will begin to form in the middle of the line. Before it does you can make a quick wrist movement upstream . . .

2. . . . lifting the middle of the line . . .

3. . . . and repositioning it upstream so that it does not drag the fly.

Bow and Arrow Cast

The bow and arrow cast is a specialty technique, useful in those situations where overhead or roll casts are impossible. It is most helpful on waters that force you to cast from brushy banks. With this technique it is possible to cast a length of line about equal to the length of the rod. Thus if your rod is 8 feet long you have an effective casting range of about 12 to 16 feet.

1. To execute the bow and arrow cast simply grasp the fly between your thumb and forefinger near the bend of the hook and put tension on the rod by pulling the fly back in bow and arrow fashion. Aim 6 inches above the spot where you want the fly to land . . .

2. . . . and let go. Over the years this cast has produced a number of large trout that I would never have had a chance at otherwise. Extreme stealth must be used, however, because you must get quite close to the fish and can easily spook it.

Reach Cast to the Right

The reach cast (to the right or left) is normally made when fishing at an angle upstream. A reach cast helps deliver a drag-free fly to the waiting trout and helps present the fly first, before the fish can see the line and leader, which may frighten it. Whether you make a reach cast to the left or right depends on the current. If you are facing upstream on the left edge of the river, you make reach casts to the left. If you are facing upstream on the right bank, you reach cast to the right. In the middle of the stream, you can make reach casts in either direction depending upon where the fish lie.

1. To reach cast to the right, make a normal overhead cast. Just as the line straightens out in the air . . .

2. . . . quickly reach to the right with your rod arm fully extended. At the same time, release line from your left hand to avoid pulling the fly off target. Your line will move to the right so that it doesn't drift over the trout's position, but your fly will float directly over the fish.

Reach Cast to the Left

1. To reach cast to the left, begin with a normal overhead cast. Just as the line straightens out in the air . . .

2. . . . quickly turn your shoulders and reach to the left with your rod arm fully extended across your body. At the same time release the line from your left hand to keep the fly on target. Your line and leader will move to the left so that they don't drift over the trout; your fly, however, will come right down the food lane.

Sidearm Cast

The sidearm cast is simply a version of the overhead cast and is used when other casts are impossible because of bankside obstacles or water currents. For example, consider a trout in fast water, resting near the bank under overhanging brush. An upstream roll cast is not practical because of the swift current. Because an overhead cast angles down on the water from above, it will either hang up in the brush or fail to deliver the fly far enough beneath the overhanging branches to reach the fish. This is the time for a sidearm cast.

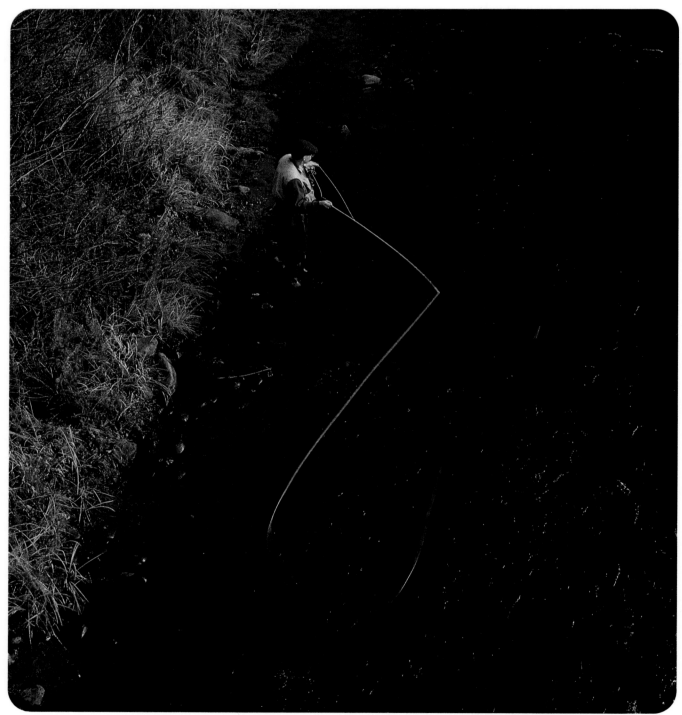

1. Cast with your rod parallel to the river. When the low backcast straightens out over the stream . . .

2. . . . punch it forward to create a tight loop . . .

3. . . . that will carry the fly beneath the brush and into the confined holding spot.

Hook Cast to the Right

A hook cast is handy for positioning the fly on the water to avoid in-stream obstructions and in preventing the fish from seeing the leader before it sees the fly. Because a hook cast involves making a sidearm cast with a hinged, finishing hook to the left or right, it is difficult to make accurately.

To execute the hook cast to the right, s-l-o-w-l-y cast sidearm, creating a very wide casting loop. On the forward delivery, no power or punch is added to the cast. Simply slow the casting stroke so that the cast is under-powered. Instead of straightening out, the leader and fly land on the water in a hook-shaped fashion. The forward delivery for the right-hook cast must be progressively slower and slower in order to set fly, leader and line down in the proper configuration.

Hook Cast to the Left

To make the hook cast to the left, it is necessary to over-power a sidearm cast, and then stop the rod abruptly. This will cause the fly to swing around and hook to the left at the end of the cast. If extreme hooking is required you can make a short haul on the line with your left hand, just before the sidearm cast begins to straighten. The haul will increase the line speed and cause the fly to swing farther to the left as it forms the hook.

Large, bushy or heavy flies on light leaders are difficult to cast with a hook to the left. The air resistance or extra weight can prevent the light leader from swinging around, or can cause it to collapse before the cast is completed.

Drop Cast

The drop cast becomes important when very selective trout are surface feeding in clear water. This cast is made from a position upstream of the fish, and by providing many feet of slack line after the cast is completed, you can deliver a drag-free dry fly downstream to the trout. Unlike the traditional upstream presentation, the drop cast allows the trout to see the fly before it sees the leader or line.

1. Make an overhead cast. When your forward cast is fully extended over the water but not touching the surface, pull the rod back gently . . .

2. . . . to slightly "spring" the line back toward you. This motion will deposit about 10 feet of slack line on the water.

3. The current will gradually straighten the slack while your fly rides downstream, drag-free, to the jaws of the waiting trout.

Had you not pulled your line back in step 2 the fly would have alighted on the water and immediately dragged in the current, a behavior that would not appeal to the trout.

The drop cast can be very accurate. Rather than standing directly upstream of the fish, move off to one side. This position will also keep the line and leader from passing over the fish at the end of the drift. Cast 5 to 10 feet upstream and beyond the rising trout. As the fly touches the water, lift your rod high and gently pull the fly back until it's in the trout's feeding lane. Then lower the rod. Drawing the fly back like this will provide the necessary slack and put the fly in position for a perfectly aligned, drag-free float.

If more line is needed to extend the drift, shake additional line out with quick side-to-side or up-and-down flips of the rod tip. Shake out this additional line before the line on the water has straightened out, since the resistance of the slack line on the water will help pull the extra line out through the guides and allow the fly to continue drifting with little or no drag.

Wiggle Cast

Few streams have uniform current flows and any time you cast a dry fly across uneven currents it will immediately begin to drag. You can prevent drag from setting in, however, by having some slack line on the water between the rod and the fly. The currents can "play" with this slack for a time, before they grab your fly and start dragging it. The more slack you have, the longer the drift.

The wiggle cast will give you this needed slack. It is designed to put slack where it's needed in fast water and to eliminate slack where it's not needed in slower water. The wiggle cast is so named because of the wiggling motion you give the rod tip after you make your forward cast. As the line is straightening in front of you, gently move the rod tip back and forth (1). Each wiggle you give the rod will send an "S" curve down the line, and these curves provide the slack line necessary to delay the onset of drag (2). Wider wiggles create larger curves; narrow wiggles make smaller ones; and more wiggles mean more "S" curves.

Wiggling the rod as you begin the forward cast will put the "S" curves closer to the leader. If you wiggle the rod later in the cast the curves will form closer to the rod. This allows you to position slack anywhere along the length of the line and put the drift of the fly back in your control.

To keep the fly from being pulled back toward you as you wiggle the rod, it is helpful to shoot some extra line at the same time. The other alternative is to cast a longer line to compensate for the distance the fly will be pulled back when you wiggle the rod.

1.

2.

Dapping

1. *In tight, brushy situations, dapping is an alternative to the bow and arrow cast. To dap, sneak into position. Carefully swing the rod and fly over the desired spot on the water and then gently lower the fly to the surface.*

2. *With advance preparation you can have some slack line available to let the fly drift down to a fish, or you can bounce the fly teasingly on the water. If a feeding trout is home and you have not disturbed it the take will be shockingly swift. For that reason it is easy to jerk the fly away from the fish and become snagged in the brush!*

Water Cast

Trout often inhabit the fast water along deep, brushy banks. Because a back cast is impossible and you can't get through the brush to use a bow and arrow cast, only the water cast will deliver the fly.

1. To make the water cast, position yourself just downstream of the trout's lie and strip out enough fly line to reach the fish. Extend the rod over the water and let the line drift with the current below you until there is maximum water tension on the line.

2. With the rod held low, make the water cast by coming forward smartly with your rod hand.

3. The tension of the water holding your line will be strong enough to flex your rod and thus propel the line, leader and fly forward . . .

4. . . . completing the cast. (We photographed this cast in a setting free of obstacles so that you could easily see the mechanics. Normally this cast is often performed on difficult water that many anglers pass by—for that reason it is often some of the best water on the stream.)

Casting into the Wind

Aside from a lack of fish, high and dirty water or a worm fisherman with a stringer of wild trout, a strong wind is probably the angler's most frustrating experience. The worst wind is one that blows head-on and should be avoided unless casts can be kept short. But even the most severe winds can be overcome with proper casting.

On streams, often you can take advantage of wind by locating casting positions where it comes from the side or from behind you. If the wind is at your back use a roll cast or a basic overhead cast with a high backcast. In cross-wind, wait for a brief let-up and then cast quickly, using a cast that keeps the fly line downwind of your body. This way you'll avoid tangling the line or hooking yourself. Don't let the wind fool you into thinking the fish aren't biting.

1. When you must cast directly into the wind use arm and wrist power to make the overhead cast as forcefully and quickly as possible. The added power and speed will create a very small casting loop that cuts into the wind more easily. At the end of the forward cast the rod should be driven down in a powerful follow-through . . .

2. . . . almost touching the water. Don't try to aim the fly two feet above the target as you would in calm conditions or the wind will blow the line back in your face. When casting into the wind drive the line, leader and fly onto the water's surface. Water disturbances caused by wind often will disguise any splash your cast makes.

Steeple Cast

The steeple cast involves an exaggerated overhead lift in which you make a conscious effort to drive the fly line up and over obstacles to your backcast—trees, brush, grass or high banks.

I use the steeple cast often because it is quicker to make than a roll cast and is more accurate. You will learn to judge these situations as your casting proficiency and river-reading improve from trip to trip.

1. With the rod arm held straight and fully extended, bring the rod up sharply, using the strength in your wrist to gain additional upward lift in the line. Stop the rod in an elevated position from 12 to 1 o'clock.

2. When the fly is well above the obstacles behind you, begin the forward cast by driving the rod down and out, parallel to the water in order to exert maximum power to the line.

Reverse Steeple Cast

The reverse steeple cast is a modified overhead cast that is very helpful when a roll cast will not provide the necessary distance or cut into the wind well enough. I also use it to keep the fly line downwind of me.

To execute this cast turn around and aim your forward cast into whatever narrow openings or breaks you can find in the brush or trees you are facing. This will provide a longer forward and a longer, easier backcast.

1. The object is to bring the forward cast high, above all the obstacles in front of you . . .

2. . . . and let your line straighten out . . .

3. . . . before making the backward power cast . . .

4. . . . as you turn slightly to follow through.

6
Presentation

You have spent many hours practicing your casting and have confidence in your new-found skill. But there is more to fishing than casting. You must read the water, select the right fly to match the food on which the fish are feeding, and most importantly, present the fly in a way that will fool fish into taking it.

The following presentations are meant as a starting point. They are not the only techniques, but understanding them will help you catch fish. As your experience grows you will add to these presentations new ones learned from your own experiments or from more experienced anglers.

The Dry Fly Drift

Dry flies are meant to float on the waters surface and are usually tied to imitate some form of insect that trout feed on. Since the dry fly drift imitates the way a natural fly floats on the water, the cast must be executed in a way that gives the fly a drag-free drift, one where the fly floats free of all movement except that caused by the current. After making the upstream cast, raise the rod or strip in line as the fly floats back toward you. This will keep the moving water from pulling on any extra line, causing the fly to drag. By keeping the extra line off the water you will also be able to set the

hook easily in any trout that takes the fly. On a cross-stream or downstream cast, mending the line or feeding out slack will extend the fly's drift past the fish without spooking them. For a more natural drift always cast a few feet upstream of feeding or holding trout and let the fly drift 3 or 4 feet past them.

The Nymph Bottom Bounce

To imitate nymphs bouncing along the stream bottom, cast a short length of line with a weighted fly upstream at a 45-degree angle to the current. If needed, adjust the weight by putting split shot on the leader 12 to 18 inches above the fly. If it snags on the bottom too often, replace it with a lighter one. As your fly line drifts back toward you lift the tip of your rod to keep the slack off the water. Follow the tip of the fly line or strike indicator with the rod. When the indicator drifts past you mend the line upstream. Then lower the rod tip as the strike indicator floats downstream, extending your drag-free drift as far as possible.

If the fly line or strike indicator are dragging on the surface the weighted fly will lift off the bottom. The float must be kept drag-free.

Whenever you notice any unusual movement of the fly

line or indicator, flip the tip of the rod up or sideways to set the hook in a trout or to free it from the bottom.

The Wet Fly Swing

Wet-fly fishing is a very effective way to search new water or to fish before a hatch when insects are swimming to the surface.

Position yourself upstream from the water you want to fish and cast your wet fly downstream and across the current. The fly should land a short distance beyond and upstream from the fish's holding water. You want the fly to swim slowly downstream, just as a natural insect would, and then swing around below you. The speed at which the fly swings down and across is controlled by adjusting your casting angle to match the speed of the current. In faster currents cast the fly more down stream, then mend upstream to slow the fly. In slower currents cast more directly across the current.

At the end of the drift lift up on the rod tip. This will rise the fly to the surface, imitating a hatching insect. You can also gently twitch the rod tip throughout the drift to imitate a struggling insect.

There is little doubt that when a fish strikes at a swinging wet fly the sharp tug will announce his presence.

The Saltwater Stalk

To fish saltwater flats with any luck it pays to go out with a local guide who understands the tides and habits of the fish you will be stalking.

Fish in shallow-water flats are very spooky and must be fished from a distance. You must be able to form tight casting loops and deliver a fly at least 60 feet with only one or two false casts in wind that might be blowing from any direction. The fly must land accurately and softly a short distance in front of the fish, with no splash of line or fly that might spook it. With this in mind practice casting a weight forward line at 60 feet or more while using only one or two false casts. Practice will enable you to concentrate more on the fishing once you're on the water and will make the experience more enjoyable for both you and your guide.

The Bass Bug Twitch

Bass bugs float on the surface or just below it. Most are large, so you will need a 7 or 8 weight slow action rod, a weight forward line and a leader designed to turn over a heavy fly.

From a boat or float tube position yourself 20 to 30 feet away from the fish's holding water and cast the bug with slow, wide loops. As soon as the bug hits the water, lower the tip of the rod so it points right at the bug and then strip in any slack line. When the bug has rested 5 or 10 seconds, twitch the end of your rod and again strip in any slack. Repeat the pause, twitch and strip until you have covered the area.

When a bass strikes, set the hook quickly by pulling hard straight back on the rod, and immediately lift the rod to keep the fish from diving back into the cover.

The Panfish Creep

Panfish seem to inhabit every lowland lake and pond in the country. They offer a good way to practice casting and have enjoyable fishing at the same time.

Use a 4 or 5 weight fly rod with a floating line and a weighted wet fly or nymph. A fly tied on a long-shank hook is easier to remove from a panfish. Though it is simpler to fish from a float tube or boat neither is really necessary. Cast to the area you wish to fish and let the fly settle for a few seconds. Begin stripping the line in at a creeping pace, about one inch per second. After 5 to 10 strips pause for a few seconds. Repeat the process, letting the fly sink deeper on each cast, until you locate the fish. If you count the number of seconds that you allow the fly to sink you can return the fly to the same depth after you catch a fish.

Panfish take the fly very softly. You should gently lift up on the rod if you sense anything unusual. If you feel no resistance lower the rod and continue fishing.

The Streamer Swing

A streamer fished on a floating line should be weighted, or have weight attached to the leader. The fly doesn't have to bounce along the bottom, but it should be close so that the trout won't have to chase it.

The cast will depend on the depth of the water being fished. With deep water, cast upstream and across from the area you want to fish so the fly will have time to sink. In shallow water, position yourself so you are upstream from the area to be covered; then cast downstream and across, so that the fly lands upstream and across from the area to be fished.

When the streamer is at the depth you want to fish, start leading the fly back to your side of the stream with the tip of the rod. Hold the rod tip low to the water, then twitch it an inch or two upstream sporadically as the fly swings across the current. The idea is to make the streamer act like an injured minnow. At the end of the swing, fish the fly back toward you with two inch strips. Vary the action you give the streamer on succeeding casts, fishing it fast, slow, or with no action.

Strikes come hard and fast and fish usually hook themselves.

The Steelhead Swing

To fly fish for summer steelhead with either a floating line or a sink tip line it is often best to allow the fly to be worked in a controlled swing through the suspected holding water. Position yourself at the top of the run, pool or tailout and cast downstream at about a 45 degree angle (more upstream if the water is slow, more downstream if the water is fast).

As soon as the fly touches the water make a quick upstream line mend to slow its progress as it cuts through the water in an arc. Try to smoothly bring the fly through the holding water so the fly will have maximum time to incite the curiosity of the steelhead. Between each cast move about two feet downstream. The colder the water becomes, the deeper and slower the fly must move. As a general rule, use a floating line for summer steelhead in water down to 48 degrees. Always use a fast sinking tip line for winter steelhead.

LEARN MORE ABOUT FLY FISHING AND FLY TYING WITH THESE BOOKS

If you are unable to find the books shown below at your local book store
or fly shop you can order direct from the publisher below.

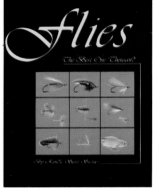

Flies: The Best One Thousand
Randy Stetzer
$24.95

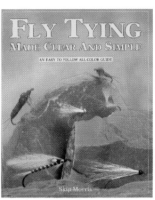

Fly Tying Made Clear and Simple
Skip Morris
$19.95 (HB: $29.95)

The Art of Tying the Dry Fly
Skip Morris
$29.95 (HB:$39.95)

Curtis Creek Manifesto
Sheridan Anderson
$7.95

American Fly Tying Manual
Dave Hughes
$9.95

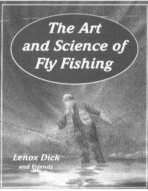

The Art and Science of Fly Fishing
Lenox Dick
$19.95

Western Hatches
Dave Hughes, Rick Hafele
$24.95

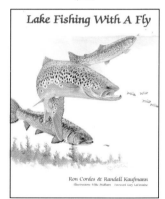

Lake Fishing with a Fly
Ron Cordes, Randall Kaufmann
$26.95

Advanced Fly Fishing for Steelhead
Deke Meyer
$24.95

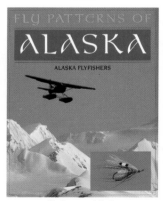

Fly Patterns of Alaska
Alaska Flyfishers
$19.95

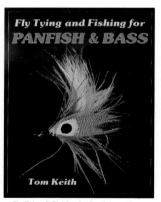

Fly Tying & Fishing for Panfish and Bass
Tom Keith
$19.95

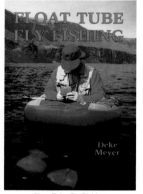

Float Tube Fly Fishing
Deke Meyer
$11.95

VISA, MASTERCARD or AMERICAN EXPRESS ORDERS CALL TOLL FREE: 1-800-541-9498
(9-5 Pacific Standard Time)

Or Send Check or money order to:

Frank Amato Publications
Box 82112
Portland, Oregon 97282

(Please add $3.00 for shipping and handling)